Love Wildly

Kayla Garrett

BookLeaf Publishing

India | USA | UK

Presentation by *BookLeaf Publishing*

Web: www.bookleafpub.com

E-mail: info@bookleafpub.com

ISBN: 9789360944599

First edition 2024

ACKNOWLEDGEMENT

I would like to acknowledge the extraordinary debt I owe to the individuals that supported me during the years through my writing journey, without them none of this would be possible. My mom Maria Garrett, my father Jeff Garrett, and of course my son Xavier Dean.

PREFACE

I hope you enjoy this collection of poems that show the purest love. If you enjoyed this book you should take a look at my other one also published by BookLeaf Publishing, "Speckle of light in the darkness". It is also a collections of poems about a young woman trying to heal her trauma after an abusive relationship.

You

The sun, moon, and the stars.
You make me feel like the whole universe just
by looking into your big blue eyes.
The moment I see you my heart beats faster and
my breathing changes.
Nervous and excitement overwhelm me, and I
lose all control.
Palms sweaty, shaky at the knees.
One single touch from you and the butterflies
awakens inside me.
Once your lips touch mine, I melt into you like
we are one.
To scared to tell you.
I felt the spark as soon as I pulled into that
parking lot and you were standing there by your
truck waiting for me to arrive.
The moment you smiled at me, the number of
times I caught you staring at me from across the
table.
Smiling like you were the luckiest man alive.
That's how you make me feel, that smile, and
those eyes make me feel like I can do anything.
That I am the sun, moon, and the stars.

Happiness

Warmth, safety, pure happiness.
Smiles, laughs, holding one another just for a while.
Felt like that was exactly where I was supposed to be.
Feel the purity of our chemistry, that is where I want to stay.
In the safety net of your strong warm embrace.

Addiction

Unconditional love not the addiction of needing
all your attention, just knowing of your love.
Feeling of your warm embrace after a horrible
day.
Your smile when times are tough, and time apart
seems too long.
Sounds of your voice makes me feel safe and
able to accomplish anything.
I know that we are both still healing from all our
past traumas and that you have a wall guarding
your heart.
But I hope that by showing my unconditional
love in return that you will know of something
so pure.
Your love is a drug that I cannot stop longing
for.
The pure addiction of its essence.

Attraction

Magnetic,
Pulling, attracting, drawing me in,
into your warmth safe haven.
Eyes glistening in the distance,
speaking to my soul.
Begging to let you in, give into your crooked
smile, how it lights up on entire room.
Laugh so radiant and contagious that it pushes
the darkness away.
Hands so rough and calloused from work but yet
so gentle on my skin.
Voice rasp, loud, full echoing into my last nerve
when you say my name.
So magnetic,
your heart dragging me in, to try and break away
at the wall surrounding your heart.
Reassuring you that I am here to stay
wholeheartedly.

Ocean

5

Should've never looked into your ocean blue
eyes.
I got lost in the pure depth of you,
looking up at the stars trying to find my way
back.
Seeing true north but still unable to leave.
Then you hit me with our first kiss and it was all
over for me.
Even with my eyes closed I could see all of you.
Fireworks raised inside me and exploded,
rattling my soul alive.
At that moment I knew you were going to be
such an amazing person in my life.
I want to live in that moment forever.

Cloud 9

Shivering, goosebumps, hair raising on the back
of my neck.
A shiver moving down my spine.
Your touch so electrifying.
Constantly retracing places your hands once
were.
A smile and gasp reach my lips with every
memory even better than the last.
Lips so soft and gentle knowing exactly where
to move next to illuminate the fire inside my
soul.
A touch so gentle, comforting, yet so strong and
firm.
Warm and tingling feelings overcomes me with
every touch and look you give.
Eyes piercing blue like the sky after a
horrendous thunderstorm, teasing me to give in.
To let you have all of me,
every inch of your skin on my body,
begging you to touch and caress,
sparking fireworks within.
Mind becoming fuzzy and lightheaded from all
of the senses being overwhelmed.
Wet and throbbing wanting so badly to feel you
inside me.

Yet so scared and vulnerable that once I give
myself over that I will fully and completely and
hysterically fall head over heels for you.
Mind and body taking over and giving in to the
temptation.
No matter how fragile and vulnerable my heart
is,
feeling you deep inside me.
Gasping, moaning, gripping for anything to
bring me back to reality.
Then I feel you throb inside me, and I see the
stars and the moon behind my eyelids before my
eyes rolled to the back of my head.
I feel every nerve and cell implode until my
back arches and I feel as if I'm floating among
the clouds.

Seasons

Orange like the leaves changing in autumn with the freckles of red and brown peeking through.
Spiral curls of golden brown hair dangling in your eyes.
Eyes lively, vibrantly blue like the sky on a cloudless day.
A smile so full of life and love that makes my heart swoon.
Praying that God has answered my prayer.
Constantly filling the room with your voice to keep the quiet at bay.
Telling me all about your family and crazy stories.
Saying all the right words.
I think about you as soon as I wake and at night right before my eyes close.
Dreaming of the strong, hardworking man that hardly has time for himself but still finds time to make me smile.
The season is changing, air becoming colder, leaves fading into orange with freckles of red.
Reminding me of you with every glance I take.
You are like the seasons abrupt, unexpected in the changes but yet so comforting in every way.
So vibrant with patience and life.
Brown and red peeking through the orange as the green fades from the leaves.

Universe

The sun, moon, and the stars;
feeling like your whole universe in just one
stare.
Seeing galaxies in your eyes.
Thinking the affection of the brightness would
last.
As the light of our star fades and implodes,
the sky becomes brighter.
Vanishing all the hurt that was caused from our
fall out.
My heart never filled the hole that you left but
once I heard from you everything changed.
You made me feel like all the stars in the
galaxies have aligned.

Tenderness

Intoxication, dizzy, numb feeling succumbs my
trembling body.
Your ever so softly touch of your hand on my
cheek as you look into my hopeful eyes.
Kissing my soft juicy lips with such gentleness
like a delicate flower about to bloom.
Moving my hair out of my face to reveal the
brightest of smiles.
Staring into each other's eyes, to ponder our next
move.
The seconds move by slowly like a snowflake
on the windowpane of an abandoned house.
No warmth or energy,
time standing still, breathing heightens, and
nerves become overwhelmed.
Eyes slowly closing to take in every second of
this moment.
Your warm breath on my neck, goosebumps
running up my arms, a shover moving down my
spine.
Not wanting this moment to end.

Unconditional

Unconditional love,
passion,
the safety net of your warm embrace.
Constantly reassuring of your intentions and
caring heart.
Ready to take on my dark damaged fragile soul,
to slowly mend the pieces back together.
Being each other's light of hope from our trouble
past.
Always concerned of my feelings, asking if I'm
okay or constantly apologizing.
You make me laugh hysterically until I snort and
tears falling down my face.
Consistently placing a smile upon my face.
Already the feeling of home within your
snuggled embrace.
My head upon your chest feeling the rise and
fall, heart beating faster with each touch.
The safest place in the world, falling hopelessly
in love with you.

Storyteller

I fell for your thoughts,
the way that you smile at me with a twinkle in
your eyes.
How you made me speechless.
I ache to hear another story,
hear the laughter hidden behind your voice.
Get lost in adventure.
I want you lying next to me,
you are caressing my face as I look into your
eyes,
running your fingers through my hair.
I fell for you.
I ache for you.
I want you.

Rainy day

You remind me of a rainy day,
the misty smell mixed with oak trees right
before the first rain fall of autumn.
The vibrant orange and red color of the leaves
before they finally let go of their home.
You remind me of the cozy warm feeling of the
first bonfire on a cold October night.
The coziness of a fuzzy blanket after dancing in
the rain.
You make me feel so warm and fuzzy.
Full of loving emotions,
constant butterflies,
and a permanent smile upon my face.
You make me feel like a worth a future I've been
longing for.
Random dances in the rain,
phone calls at 2 am,
star gazing in an empty field,
and a kiss that sets my soul on fire.
You make me feel again.

Sky full of Stars

When you look up at the sky full of stars, do you
think of us?
Where our life could've been,
full of love and laughter.
Surrounded by the sound of grasshoppers
playing a melody while the wind blows through
the field of possibilities.
If I wouldn't have reached out to you, I would
have never known how you feel.
How my heart was still hurting for you.
How one look into those eyes, I knew that I still
loved you.
Like the sun loves the moon,
how Hades loves Persephone.
My life has forever changed because of you.

Wheat Field

Dreaming of wheat fields and lavender.
The first rise of the sun after a tremendous
rainstorm.
The smell of oak in the distance.
Sun glistening off the dewy grass.
A warm touch upon your cheek, one single tear
falling.
Looking across the vast fields, to see my dream
just an arm's reach away.
Do I take the leap of faith?
Finally having the love God has prepared for,
with the man I see my entire future within his
blue eyes.
His soft ringlets of red curls casting a glow from
the sun to look like changing leaves in the fresh
months of autumn.
He looks into my eyes and says,"imagine a
wheat field and just breath. Everything will get
better."
Thats when I knew to jump.

Home

In a field of wheat,
sun shining upon the rolling hills,
wind blowing my hair free from my face as tears
run down my face,
staring at the sheer beauty of it all.
Anticipating the walk to you.
A crooked grin upon your face, eyes so bright
blue that it set your body of fire.
The walk to you is long and nerving, wondering
if this is all a dream or a wish come true.
Thinking this is finally close to the beautiful
beginning of a chapter full of love and
adventure.
Proceeding on the walk to you I see
constellations and count the stars until I get to
you.
Shooting stars and the glow of the moon,
brighten as we approach each other in an
embrace as you whisper, I love you,
Thats when I realize that I am finally home.

Sunset

Watching the sunset in the field of wildflowers,
sun falling lower and lower into the horizon.
Until blackness overtakes the sky.
Gazing at the star illuminating the cloudless sky.
Dreaming of the time I first heard you laugh.
How that smile brought so much joy,
how by a single look I knew that this could be it.
This could be what is written in the stars,
galaxies abroad,
lifetimes after lifetimes.
What people read about in romance novels.

Real love

18

Real love does not meet you when you are at
your best but when you are a complete mess.
It happens when you least expect it to.
It will appear out of thin air, and you will
understand why it never worked with anyone
else.

Keep swimming

I kept moving forward not because I wanted to.
No trust me I didn't want to.
I was willing to give up on this so-called idea of
love, because for me it was never anything like
it was portrayed in all the romance novels that
I've read.
I kept moving forward because I deserved to
know what it is like to be loved properly.
And God has sent me on that path to
unconditional love with a man that holds himself
to high regard and will not let you fall or fail in
his presence.

First

You were the first person I felt wildly unsure of,
that was the scariest part about falling in love
with you.
The fact I had no idea where this path would
take us,
but at the same time, I knew exactly why I had
to.

www.ingramcontent.com/pod-product-compliance
Lightning Source LLC
Chambersburg PA
CBHW071247140726
47996CB00007B/2785